CW01095486

DUSUM KHYENPA'S SONGS AND TEACHINGS

A VARIETY OF SONGS AND TEACHINGS FROM THE FIRST KARMAPA'S COLLECTED WORKS

TONY DUFF
PADMA KARPO TRANSLATION COMMITTEE

First edition, November 2008
ISBN: 978-9937-9031-4-1

Janson typeface with diacritical marks
Designed and created by Tony Duff
Tibetan Computer Company
http://www.tibet.dk/tcc

Produced, Printed, and Published by
Padma Karpo Translation Committee
P.O. Box 4957
Kathmandu
NEPAL

Web-site and e-mail contact through:
http://www.tibet.dk/pktc
or search Padma Karpo Translation Committee on the web.

CONTENTS

INTRODUCTION

This is a small book of the songs and teachings of the first Karmapa, Dusum Khyenpa [1110–1193]. Dusum Khyenpa was a great yogin who studied under Gampopa and attained to great realization. Some years after his death, he was recognized as the first incarnation of the Karmapas who were then heads of the Karma Kagyu lineage of Tibetan Buddhism.

All the teachings here are taken from the *Collected Works* of Dusum Khyenpa. Dusum Khyenpa's *Collected Works* is very rare which is striking given that he is one of the very important early figures of the Kagyu Lineage. My committee recently obtained a copy and has rescued it from near extinction. Our new, electronic edition of the *Collected Works* is available from our web-site whose address is on the copyright page at the front of the book.

The first teaching in this book is Dusum Khyenpa's transmission of a specific Mahamudra teaching that came from India, called "Mahamudra the Thunderbolt". It is not an explanation of the teaching but a straightforward transmission of the teaching itself. As with so many of these teachings that came from India, it is very short and pithy.

The rest of the selections in this book are from the collection of dohas in the *Collected Works*. Dohas are songs spontaneously sung out of and about realization. They are particularly important in the Kagyu lineage where they are one of the very important sources of teaching for the followers of the lineage. When we first obtained the *Collected Works* of Dusum Khyenpa, we expected that the doha section would be extensive and intended to produce a major book of the first Karmapa's dohas for the many people who have faith in the Karmapa and his teachings. Unfortunately, it was not the case; the doha section of the *Collected Works* is very short, containing a total of eight dohās altogether.

The first doha is a very straightforward lineage supplication, not particularly different from many other supplications found in the writings of the Kagyu lineage so we did not translate it. The remaining seven dohas consist of a letter to a disciple in the form of a doha that was found and included in the collection and six dohas heard by the person who wrote them down. Note that doha II contains another, specific Mahamudra transmission from ancient India, the teaching called "The Three Vajra Words".

If you are interested in the life and works of the Karmapas, you might also like to read our forthcoming book on the Gampopa's interviews with his major yogin disciples. Nearly half the book is taken up with the question and answer sessions of Gampopa and Dusum Khyenpa. When you read what Gampopa has to say, you can easily recognize and often understand better much of what Dusum Khyenpa talks about in his dohas. We are sure you would find it interesting.

Our Supports for Study

I have been encouraged over the years by all of my teachers and gurus to pass on some of the knowledge I have accumulated in a lifetime dedicated to the study and practice, primarily through the Tibetan Buddhist tradition, of Buddhism. On the one hand they have encouraged me to teach. On the other hand, they are concerned that, while many general books on Buddhism have been and are being published, there are few books that present the actual texts of the tradition. They and many other, closely involved people have encouraged me to make and publish high quality translations of individual texts of the tradition.

In general, we have published a wide range of books that present the important literature of Tibetan Buddhism. In particular, the author of this book, Dusum Khyenpa, was one of the key figures connected with the transmission of the Mahamudra teaching in Tibet and we have published many of the important texts of that system, with each one carefully selected to inform about a particular aspect of that teaching. We especially recommend reading our *Gampopa's Mahamudra, The Five-Part Mahamudra of the Kagyus* in conjunction with this; it not only lays out the Kagyu Mahamudra teaching very clearly and extensively but contains other texts from Dusum Khyenpa's tradition.

All in all, you will find many books both for free and for sale on our web-site, all of them prepared to the highest level of quality. Many of our books are available not only on paper but as electronic editions that can be downloaded, and all of them are prepared to the highest level of quality. We encourage you to look at our web-site to see what we have; the address is on the copyright page at the front of this book. Major book sellers also carry our paper editions.

It has also been a project of ours to make tools that non-Tibetans and Tibetans alike could use for the study and translation of Tibetan texts. As part of that project, we prepare electronic editions of Tibetan texts in the Tibetan Text input office of the Padma Karpo Translation Committee and make them available to the world. Tibetan texts are often corrupt so we make a special point of carefully correcting our work before making it available through our web-site. Thus, our electronic texts are not careless productions like most Tibetan texts found on the web but are highly reliable editions that can be used by non-scholars and scholars alike. Moreover, many of the texts are free. The texts for this book are available from us as electronic editions as part of our electronic edition of the *Collected Works of Dusum Khyenpa*.

Our electronic texts can be read, searched, and so on, using our Tibetan software. The software can be used to set up a reference library of these texts and then used to read and even research them quickly and easily. The software, called TibetD and TibetDoc, has many special features that make it useful not only for reading but also for understanding and even translating texts. One key feature is that you can highlight a Tibetan term in a text then look it up immediately in

Dusum Khyenpa, The first Karmapa

any of our electronic dictionaries. We suggest the highly acclaimed *Illuminator Tibetan-English Dictionary* as the best dictionary for the purpose. As with all of our publications, the software and electronic texts can be obtained from our web-site whose address is on the copyright page at the front of the book.

Lotsawa Tony Duff,
Swayambunath,
Nepal,
4th November 2008

A SHORT BIOGRAPHY OF THE FIRST KARMAPA DUSUM KHYENPA

The first Karmapa Dusum Khyenpa [1110–1193 AD] was one of the eighteen foremost disciples of Gampopa. He was born into a Buddhist family in Ratay in East Tibet and received his first dharma teachings from his father, who gave him teachings on Mahakali.

He continued his education with other Buddhist teachers in East Tibet and at the age of 20 took ordination with a preceptor of Atisha's Kadampa tradition. Following that, he moved to Central Tibet where the Kadampa teachers of the time were concentrated. Once there, he spent twelve years studying and practising sutra and tantra with masters of the area, including Kyabpa Chokyi Senge and Patsab Lotsawa Nyima Trag[1].

At the age of thirty he went to Gampopa's monastery called Daglha Gampo. Gampopa saw that Dusum Khyenpa was a great bodhisatva[2] but made him study and practise the basic practices of the Kadampa tradition called "Stages of the Path"[3]. He also made him study sutra philosophy extensively.

After that, Gampopa empowered him into the mandala of Hevajra and gave him the necessary instructions to go with it. Dusum Khyenpa then spent four years practising it.

After that, he was then given the inner practices of the Kagyu tradition that Milarepa had taught Gampopa. Dusum Khyenpa also went to Rechungpa and other students of Milarepa for teachings. Milarepa mainly practised Fierce Heat[4] combined with Mahamudra, as did Gampopa following him, and Dusum Khyenpa, too. Dusum Khyenpa rapidly progressed in the practice.[5]

Dusum Khyenpa had great natural ability for meditation and spent many years meditating in mountain caves. At one point, he spent months in a hut so tiny that the meditation posture, cross-legged and erect, was the only possible form of occupancy.

When Gampopa died, Dusum Khyenpa returned to Gampopa's Daglha Gampo monastery in order to pay homage to his teacher. While he was there, he had a vision one night of his guru[6]. As a result of the vision, he knew that it was the appropriate time to follow one of Gampopa's last instructions to him, which was to go to Gampo Gangra and practice Mahamudra there. He did so and gained the final realization of enlightenment there. His enlightenment was celebrated by the dakinis who made him a gift of a crown made from their hair. The crown is said to have been thenceforth always present, though invisible, above the heads of all the Karmapas. After that, amongst other things, Dusum Khyenpa prophesied that he would live to the age of 84, in order to benefit the Dharma, and sentient beings.

At forty-four, Dusum Khyenpa left Central Tibet to return to the region of his birth. There, he spent the thirty-nine years until his death in establishing three thriving monasteries, sharing the Kagyu teachings, and training his students. At the age of 58, he founded the Gampo Nenang monastery. Later he founded the Karma Gon monastic complex, and at the age of 74, he established another monastery at Tsurphu. Tsurphu is situated in the Tolung valley, which leads to the Brahmaputra valley, and is near Lhasa. It became the principal seat of the Karmapas for the next seven hundred years.

Several of the great disciples of Gampopa passed the teachings on to their disciples which led to the many different Kagyu lineages that exist today. Dusum Khyenpa's lineage became known as the Karma Kagyu. Dusum Khyenpa had many great disciples and of these, he chose the one called Drogon Rechen, meaning "The great repa who is protector to all beings" to be his lineage holder. In addition, he wrote a prediction letter that gave very clear indications about his coming rebirth and gave that letter to Drogon Rechen. This was the first time that such a thing had been done in Tibetan Buddhism and it started the whole Tibetan "tulku" system where a being takes a deliberate rebirth in a future life in order to carry on the work of the predecessor. Dusum Khyenpa was very famous for this.

Dusum Khyenpa passed away, just as he had predicted, at the age of 84. It was reported that his heart and tongue remained intact in the funeral pyre, despite the intense heat, which is one sign of a very great being. It was also reported that his bones were left behind in shapes of buddhas. This is another sign of a very great being.

Notes:

1. These were both very highly regarded teachers of their time.

2. This is the correct spelling according to the whole Tibetan tradition despite the usual spelling of bodhisattva seen in Western books.

3. This is genre of teachings that became a very important part of the Kadampa teaching system. It started with a seminal text that Atisha wrote for his Tibetan disciples that taught in this style. Atisha's text was called called "Lamp of the Path to Enlightenment".

4. Tib. gtum mo. Tummo, literally meaning "The fierce one" refers to the practice of development of fierce heat. The practice has often been called inner heat but that misses out on key meanings of the term.

5. Many details of his practice of these two key practices of the Kagyu are reported in the interviews that Dusum Khyenpa had with Gampopa and these can be read in our forthcoming book on Gampopa's interviews.

6. The first of the dohas in Doha VIII tells the story of this time.

MAHAMUDRA, THE THUNDERBOLT

He said this.

"Namo Guru.

There are four parts to "Mahamudra, The Thunderbolt":

1. what it is in three parts;
2. the meaning of the words in four parts;
3. ways of going astray in three parts;
4. the technique for resting in it in four parts.

What it is in three parts:

1. non-contrivance of mind;
2. lack of accomplishment through conceptual efforts;
3. knowledge in mind of sensations[1].

At the time of path, non-contrivance is the view, lack of accomplishment through effort[2] is the meditation, and knowledge in mind of sensations is the conduct. At the time of fruition, non-contrivance is dharmakaya, lack of accomplishment through effort is sambhogakaya, and knowledge in mind of sensations is nirmanakaya. Thus, non-contrivance is like a golden ground, lack of accomplishment through effort is the gold being free of all oxidation, and knowledge in mind of sensations is like the gold showing various reflections on its surface but not wavering from being gold in substance.

The meaning of the words in four parts:

1. afflictions[3] are not to be abandoned; it is one's own mind.
2. antidotes are not to be applied; it is not something other than mind.
3. suchness is not to be cultivated by meditation; it is the consistent with identification[4].
4. if mind[5] is comprehended, it is wisdom; it is not that buddha has to be sought elsewhere.

The ways of going astray in three parts:

1. aiming for buddha as something spiritually higher is to stray;
2. thinking that there has to be bad births down below is to stray; and
3. attachment to these appearances, immediate and fresh, is to stray.

The technique for resting in it in four parts:

1. just like letting the pure part of water appear by not raking up the mud, so rest in mind left uncontrived;
2. just like the sun itself is free of clouds, so rest in the sixfold group left loose[6];

3. just like the trace of a bird flying, rest in rigpa[7] without support[8];
4. just like a flowing river, at any time you are engaged in whatever conduct, rest in non-distraction[9].

The example[10] is that, in the world when a thunderbolt descends, there is nothing that can prevent it, and similarly, when you comprehend the meaning of Mahamudra, it is not possible to be obscured by any thing or conceptual apparatus at all."

That was "Mahamudra, The Thunderbolt", spoken by Lord Dusum Khyenpa. ITHI ཨྠིཿ[11]

Notes:

1. This is a particular way of talking found in the Mahamudra system. Mahamudra does not mean an absence of knowledge. It is not merely no-thought dharmakaya. This point gets at the need to maintain the knowing aspect of mind.

2. Here effort is a word that specifically means conceptually driven efforts.

3. Often referred to as emotions in Western language but the Buddha specifically used the word "affliction" and explained that emotions, even the apparently good ones of love and so forth, all cause enmeshment in cyclic existence and therefore are afflictions.

4. The suchness of reality is not something to be newly produced and then developed rather, since it already exists, it simply has to be identified and then acquainted with.

5. Mind here means samsaric mind. If it is comprehended for what it actually is, then its nature also will be known and that nature is wisdom. Full recognition of one's own wisdom is enlightenment.

6. The six-fold group is the sum total of consciousness that we humans have. We have six different kinds of consciousness. Leaving them loose means to leave them "to hang out" just as they are, without any attempt to restrict or change them.

7. For more on rigpa, see the glossary.

8. A bird's trace in the sky disappears immediately it has happened. Similarly, rigpa knows but, having none of the complex apparatus of samsaric mind with it, produces none of the traces that would lead to samsaric existence.

9. The image of a flowing river is one of the key metaphors used to teach conduct at the higher levels of the Mahamudra teaching. Essentially, the sense consciousness are allowed to flow on but without any of the interference of dualistic mind. In that way, all behaviour happens but without any un-enlightened aspect to it.

10. The traditional way of giving a teaching is to introduce a subject, give an explanation of it, and to end with an example to illustrate it.

11. ITHI is a mark of the Secret Mantra system. Generally speaking, it indicates that this is a profound secret not to be passed on lightly.

DOHA II

This is a letter sent to one of his disciples containing the foremost instruction[1] *for a particular transmission of Mahamudra called "The Three Vajra Words". There is a fair amount of subtlety packed into just a few words…*

OṂ SVĀSTI

I pay homage with admiring devotion to the
Medicine that cleanses impure body, speech, and mind,
To the supreme lamp that illuminates
The gloom of samsara with its three realms.[2]

The countless ones who go to buddhahood
On arrival do totally manifest that state for others.
Wherever they are born, they show delight in dharma.
Whoever they associate with, they protect the poor and destitute.
Their compassion is not contrived but a naturally occurring kind.
For the sake of migrators, they practise.

They are totally beautified by the ornaments of the seven jewels[3].
Their spheres of loving kindness and compassion,
Give equal importance to friends and enemies alike.
They have utterly abandoned favouring some and saying nice words for gain.
They truly delight in dharma without the falsity of saying one thing and thinking another.
Such is the character of the Great Vehicle family[4].

Attach no importance to this impermanent life:
Rainbows so vivid in the sky
Disappear and are gone in an instant;
Flowing rivers and frost on the ground
Fade away in a moment.
A single session of dreaming
At the time of waking is merely a recollection;
This appearance, the confusion of the six types of migrators[5],
Is un-collapsed grasping at a self—
Cut the root and the confusion is removed.
Cultivate emptiness having a core of compassion
And the two aims—of oneself and others—
Will be fulfilled, there is no doubt about it.

There are the phenomena of samsara and nirvana.
You engage in the confusion of the yoga of one's own mind[6] but
When mind is understood to be like space, the confusion is alleviated,
And that is the Middle Way divorced from the two extremes.

Mind appearing as samsara and nirvana is Mind Only
And that is valid cognition achieved through cutting exaggeration.
Bliss without grasped identification is mother tantra;
Luminosity without grasping is father tantra[7].
Every view is complete with the above whereby
It is the oral instruction of command Great Completion.
If realization such as that is aroused,
The unsatisfactoriness of samsara with its three realms is pacified,
And thus the one called "Pacifier[8]" is also dealt with there[9].
Samsara and nirvana and
Grasped and grasping[10] every single bit of it
Is the supremacy of transcendence of rational mind[11] and divorce from elaboration[12].
Realize emptiness and compassion inseparable
And you have the three anthologies of dohas[13].
No matter which particular of the path of method is considered,
This is the oral instruction for giving rise to it.
For the three pitakas of the Word[14] and the four sections of tantra
This is the explanation through which they are to be understood.
No matter which oral instruction is given
There must be devotion to the guru, and
The six migrators must be considered with compassionate activity, and
Development stage must be meditated on like turning on a light[15], and
Resting in mind's state must be cherished[16].

You mentioned the three sets of oral instructions[17] so
This, the foremost instruction[18] of the Three Vajra Words,
Which is not allowed to be written in words,
Is given to you, because you, a being who has faith,
Stays only in accord with dharma;
Thus the lord guru who accepts the dakinis' tolerance[19],
The precious Khampa[20],
Sends this letter to you, Yondag Sherab Khar.

Notes:

1. Skt. upadeśha, foremost instructions; see glossary.

2. That is a homage to his guru, Gampopa.

3. The Seven Jewels of the Noble Ones.

4. This is a standard description of the qualities of the bodhisattvas, the beings who follow the Great Vehicle, which he has inserted into the doha.

5. Hell beings, pretas, animals, humans, demi-gods, and gods.

6. When you engage in the meditation of resting in the actuality of your own mind through Mahamudra, Maha Ati, Maha Madhyamika or whatever, it is a practice done within confusion, so is a confusion practice. If the practice destroys the confusion, then ...

7. "Grasped identification" means the process of knowing something dualistically. In that case, the items of consciousness are known in a process of conceptual identification and there is grasping at a self with it. If the grasping is removed then the dualistic aspect of the identification collapses. One still knows this and that but the knowing, being freed from the grasped identification is now a flow of bliss. Mother tantra emphasizes

passion and bliss as the way to arrive at the non-dual state. Father tantra emphasizes anger and emptiness as the way to arrive at the non-dual state.

The two terms are the keynote of how the tantras describe the operation of dualistic mind and he has cleverly woven them into his explanation. Grasped identification is a process of dualistic mind in which a non-existent object is grasped at as being real and "identified" conceptually as such and such thing. If you take the bliss of mother tantra to be a real thing in this way then you have missed the point. If not, then you have the point. Father tantra is mainly concerned with emptiness; if you drop the grasping then the emptiness appears.

8. Tib. zhi byed gcod. Pacifier is an abbreviation of "Pacifier, the Cutter" which is commonly known by its Tibetan name, Chod.

9. All phenomena are included within samsara and nirvana. If you get to the emptiness of your own mind, then that is the final result. The practice and the result are described in various ways through Madhyamaka, Chittamatra, Maha Ati, Chod (which is actually known as "Pacifier"), and so on. In short he shows how this one point accomplishes the words of all views and practices.

10. See grasped-grasping in the glossary.

11. See rational mind in the glossary.

12. This is a common way of talking in Indian language which has then been brought into Tibetan. It sounds wrong in English but works like this. There is something deluded and thus not so good—he mentions four things. Those things have a core to them which is non-deluded and thus is their excellence; he points out the excellences which are transcendence of rational mind and also freedom from elaboration (which actually means the same as the first because elaboration is the hallmark of rational mind—get rid of one and you get rid of the other). These excellences found within something not so good are and traditionally called their

"glory" and also their "supreme aspect" or "supremacy".

13. The Kagyu lineage puts great emphasis on the dohas of Saraha as ways of understanding the meaning of Mahamudra. All of Saraha's dohas are gathered into three sets, called the "Three Anthologies of Dohas".

14. The Buddha Word of sutra.

15. Tib. wal gyis. This means that something is known and seen as though a light were turned on in a dark room. Pop! There is the deity, clear and totally distinct as though a light were just turned on to show it.

16. That is, completion stage must be put together with development stage.

17. In the original letter to Dusum Khyenpa, we presume.

18. Skt. upadeśha, see glossary.

19. Means that he is one who knows of and teaches the Vajra Vehicle within which one must align oneself with the messengeresses of wisdom, the dakinis.

20. Dusum Khyenpa was from Kham, so he was sometimes referred to this way, including by himself.

DOHA COLLECTION III

This doha is a spontaneously sung prayer of auspiciousness. It goes through the qualities of guru, yidam, and dharma protectors.

༄༅། །ཨོཾ་སྭ་སྟི། སྤྲུལ་སྐུ་བླ་མ་བྱོན་པ་ཡིས། །འགྲོ་བ་གང་ཟག་ལས་ཅན་ཀུན། །དངོས་འཛིན་གདོན་ལས་སྒྲོལ་མཛད་པའི། །བླ་མ་རྣམས་ཀྱི་བཀྲ་ཤིས་ཤོག །ཤེས་རབ་རང་བཞིན་རྗེ་བཙུན་མ། །བསྐྱེ་བའི་རང་བཞིན་ཚུལ་གྱིས····

OṂ SVĀSTI

The guru who has come in the form of a tulku
Liberates all the worthy beings[1]
From negative forces that come from taking things to be
real[2];
May the goodness of the gurus be present!

The Jetsunma whose nature is prajñā[3]

Through her manifested nature of love
Is the lady who leads migrators to emancipation;
May the goodness of the Jetsunma be present[4]!

In half lotus posture of magnificent pose
She is seated on sun and moon seat showing her
Possession of upāya and prajñā;
May the goodness of the Wish-fulfilling Goddess be present[5]!

Deep green body and brilliant face,
Beautified with the jeweled ornaments and Doshal necklace[6],
Right and left hands hold the utpala signifying protection from fear;
May the goodness of the supreme consort[7], Tara, be present[8]!

When meditated on with respect
The secret mantra is fully expressed and
The four activities[9] are accomplished;
May the goodness of the yidam deity be present!

Meeting again with it[10] in the future then
Becoming of the same nature with it resulting further
In the activity of guiding migrators[11];
May such goodness of inseparability be present!

Commanded by the Sugata[12] and
Witnessed by the Owner of the Secret[13]
They committed to protect the teaching;
May the goodness of the Dharma Protectors be present!

Guru, yidam, dharma protectors
Never be separated from me for so much as an instant and,
Through the goodness come from turning back ordinary discursive thoughts,
May all goodness and welfare be present!

Notes:

1. Worthy beings here are ones who have accumulated the merit needed to receive and practise the guru's teachings.

2. All negative forces are external projections that come from taking things to be real.

3. The yidam is mentioned as Jetsunma, meaning Vajrayogini in this case, and the two manifestations of her that were most popular in Tibet—White and Green Tara—are also given their own verses.

4. This verse is referring to Vajrayogini.

5. This verse is referring to White Tara.

6. There are three specific necklaces worn by women (and men, too) in ancient Indian culture. These necklaces appear in the earliest histories and spiritual works of India and are not particularly Buddhist. However, they also appear in the Buddhist tantric iconography as part of the eight jeweled ornaments worn by sambhogakaya deities. The first necklace is a very short necklace that hangs just under the throat; it is literally called a "throat necklace". The second one hangs down to breast level. It might or might not have precious stones on it. The third one hangs all the way down to the navel, or so, and has a unique and immediately recognizable design. There is a specific design that appears in three places on the necklace and this design is studded with gems of various sorts (usually three gems to each of the three

instances of the design). The name "do shal" is the Tibetan word that indicates the "various gemstones" within this third necklace. As a matter of interest, all three necklaces are still worn today, in an everyday way, by Hindu woman in India and Nepal.

7. … of the buddhas …

8. This verse is referring to Green Tara.

9. … pacifying, and so on …

10. … the yidam …

11. … to enlightenment …

12. Buddha Shakyamuni.

13. Owner of the Secret is the standard name for Vajrapani given that the Sugata, that is the Buddha himself, appointed Vajrapani as the governor in charge of the entire Secret Mantra Vehicle for the duration of Buddha Shakyamuni's teachings. The Buddha explained that he did this because he, as the leader of the monastic community, could not afford to show a Secret Mantra face to the world; if he did so, the monks and nuns would not be able to follow him.

DOHA IV

The precious guru was in Phenyul where he had been practising purely, starting in the summer and continuing on through the winter. Later he said that this doha had sprung up at that time[1].

"A beggar's thoughts come forth like this.
Knowing that samsara has no essence,
I'm free of the rational mind that builds the fence of the eight dharmas[2].
There is no turning back from nirvana yet
I'm free of rational mind's accomplishment through effort[3].
Discovering buddha in my own mind,
I'm free of the rational mind that wants siddhi[4].
The nature of thoughts being dharmakaya,
I'm free from the rational mind that judges them as good and bad.
Becoming and peace being non-dual are realized as one,
I'm free from the rational mind that distinguishes different bases[5].
The fourfold mudra shines forth as one experience[6],

I'm free from the rational mind with the duality of stopping and producing[7].
The two truths being inseparable are realized as one,
I'm free from the rational mind that has the five-path journey to tread[8].
Mindness has been seized as my own dharma seat[9],
I'm free from the rational mind that thinks of a place to be entered.
The realization of "Knowing one liberates all" has been brought forth,
I'm free from the rational mind that engages in hearing[10].
Form shines forth as illusory body,
I'm free from the rational mind that grasps at something to be cherished.
"Sounds are to be apprehended as empty" has been understood so
"Denigration and adulation are confusion" has been understood[11].
The dharmatā that comes with resting in one's own place is evident,
I'm free from the rational mind that makes a distinction between session and not[12].
This is what I have in my mind;
Son, you too, should develop such understanding."

Notes:

1. Rational mind is the specific term used to indicate the mind that is active and engages in dualities. For the most part, it is a "bad" word in the Kagyu and Nyingma traditions; rational mind is the "bad guy" who is to be removed. This is a story of one man's practice and his removal of the bad guy. See the glossary

for more on rational mind.

2. Eight worldly dharmas, which are the wall erected to keep away reality.

3. Rational mind can only accomplish something through conceptual, dualistic effort.

4. Most of us dualistically look forward to attainment but when you find buddha in your own mind, that kind of rational-minded search for attainment disappears.

5. This is a technical way of talking in Buddhist philosophy. When the sameness of becoming (samsara) and peace (nirvana) are investigated—a major point in buddhist philosophy—one argument is that the base of each is different so they cannot be the same. When you realize the reality of it, they are both empty and so there is no difference of basis.

6. This is referring to Mahamudra when it is approached through a path comprised of a sequence of four yogas. Mahamudra itself is a single experience whereas the four yogas of Mahamudra are a stepwise attainment of that experience. Even though there are four mudras in this way to Mahamudra, there is only one direct experience of it.

7. Mahamudra practiced as a fourfold journey is initially practised with the rational mind that thinks there is something not to be done and something to be accomplished in the meditation. Later, when the full meaning is realized, the dualistic need for leaving aside one thing in favour of another is seen as futile.

8. When fictional truth and superfactual truth are known to be flip sides of the coin, there is none of the five-path journey that was laid out in the Prajnaparamita sutras to be undertaken. See the glossary for explanations of fictional and superfactual truth.

9. Tib. sems nyid. Mindness is one of many names for the essence of samsaric mind. On the path, the practitioner continu-

ally engages mindness rather than mind. The practitioner takes his dharma seat within that mindness and because of it eventually reaches enlightenment.

10. There is a famous saying "Knowing one liberates all". According to Karmapa Rangjung Dorje, if you realize Mahamudra, you have full omniscience, so nothing else needs to be learned. If that happens, there is no need to engage in "hearing", which is the first of the three prajnas, the effort made to go out and hear about something so that it could be understood.

11. When sufficient practice has actually brought a person to the point where sounds are experienced as being empty, then the things of adulation and so on which are part of the fundamental confusion of life in samsara are understood for what they are.

12. When you rest in mindness, the duality of a meditation and non-meditation disappears.

DOHA V

It is reported that the Jetsun Rinpoche Physician told him, “You should go to meditate at the border of Tibet and Mon[1]" and that, following that, he acted as the personal monk of the king of Mon and stayed in the mountains of Mon at which time a companion said, “Please sing a doha for us”. It is said that this doha sprung up:

“I pay homage to the lord gurus.
I take refuge in the needed, kindly ones.
The mountains on that side are Mon mountains,
The mountains on this side are Tibetan mountains,
At the border of Mon and Tibet,
In the kingdom without end
The yogin without reference[2] wanders,
Roving the mountain tracts without something to protect[3].
So far, a tune to go with this did not arise
But, faced with the discipline of doing it,
I can now put a tune to it![4]

Those mountains over there are Mon mountains:

There's been no possibility of going there up till now;
Thus I understand the limit of nirvana.
These mountains here are Tibetan mountains:
The various concepts of samsaric mind are the causes
Of samsara; I understand its limit.
At the border of Mon and Tibet,
The kingdom without end,
Is understood to be the buddha realm.
The yogin without reference wanders,
Roving the mountain tracts without something to protect;
I understand that the eight dharmas are to be overpowered.
If you are not capable of roving the mountain tracts, then
By gathering space be not gathered!
By apprehending a breeze be not apprehended!
By looking at mindness be not seeing!
By preventing the sixfold group be not prevented[5]! and
then,
If you meditate, let your awareness remain in its own way
or,
If you destroy, let your awareness go its own way![6]
Being without clinging to samsara-nirvana is the good view;
Being without separation from no thought is the good
meditation;
Being natural arising without effort is the good conduct;
Being with clinging and desire purified into space is the
good fruition.
If you realize such meaning as that,
Various amazing tunes will come,
Divorce from fear of death will come,
Samsara going to self-liberation will come.
Accept this offered tune, Lord Guru!
Virtuous ones expert in the meaning, please pay attention!

Make your minds glad, all seated here!"

Notes:

1. The Jetsun is his guru, Gampopa. Mon was the name for the area later known as Bhutan.

2. "Without end" means that enlightenment, once obtained, is unceasing. "Without reference" means absence of the reference points that are a fundamental part of the operation of rational mind. It effectively means that he is without dualistic mind.

3. "Something to protect" here and later on means that he has no need of face-saving devices in the company of other people; he acts according to what his developed wisdom tells him and not according to what he might do to keep other people happy. If you do what keeps other people happy, it is a kind of pretense done for protecting one's own reputation or whatever else might be obtained from the other people. This is often translated as "without pretense" but that leads to a misunderstanding of what this is actually about.

4. The preamble has set the scene. It contains something interesting; he starts the song but a tune is not forthcoming but then, here, in the middle of the song, a tune suddenly appears so he starts the song over again. In the Tibetan text, you can see that he "gets into it" at that point and the power of the song is much greater from that point on.

5. A series of four things: do the conventional thing and transcend it so that one is outside of duality, for example, look at mind's essence and see what cannot be seen which is called not seeing; gather the space of emptiness and so go to the uncompounded state of being in emptiness; fo what you have to do to stop the flow of the sixfold consciousnesses and in doing so go to the state in which they flow without dualistic mind's intervention and

hence need no prevention; and so on.

6. Destruction of meditation to get to the real meditation is one of the Kagyu Mahamudra meditation instructions.

DOHA VI

Then Dusum Khyenpa went to where the guru[1] was and the guru said to him, "So, you've been to Sharmey Gangkar". He replied, "I went there. I stayed for the three summer months. Provisions were thin so, in order to be able to get provisions, I went and stayed below the gonpa there. I had thought things over and it occurred to me, "What's this! I have special oral instructions. I know how to survive using Essence Extraction[2]. I have met the sort of guru who is a buddha. I have given rise to a special level of experience and realization in my mindstream". With that, this doha sprung up."

"I've a precious guru who has the lineage,
One who can fulfil the desires and needs of fortunate
    disciples,
From whom impartial blessings appear
So if my faith and devotion are small, I'm no good!

You showed me the king of oral instructions, channels and
    winds,
From the king of Secret Mantra, mother tantra,

So if mere bliss-warmth blazes in my body,
In a pea-sized meditation, I'm no good!

If I see the father's kindness as small, I degrade myself;
I've only three woolen threads to my name but
I have the oral instructions of Fierce Heat's spontaneous
presence[3].
If ice worries me, I'm no good[4]!

I have no possessions for my own use
So can't support any faithful ones but
I know how to survive using Essence Extraction
So if food worries me, I'm no good!

The suffering of cyclic existence till now has been hard to
bear
So now that I have met the precious one
If my determination for one-pointed practice
Is weak, I'm no good!

I am to practise according to the guru's command;
Even if a steady realization does not occur
I have the oral instructions of the three bardos[5]
So if I'm afraid of death, I'm no good!"

Notes:

1. Gampopa.

2. Tib. chud len. Essence Extraction is a practice in which the various energies in the environment are taken in and absorbed. One form of the practice, when well accomplished, allows the

practitioner to survive on this energy with very little or no physical food being needed.

3. He not only has the instructions on Fierce Heat but also has the instructions on Mahamudra to go with it. The two together are a particularly effective and complete path to enlightenment.

4. Anyone with any good development of Fierce Heat will be able to sit in ice and snow without concern.

5. The bardo instructions of the Six Yogas of Naropa divide travel through the bardo into three phases each of which can be used to gain enlightenment.

DOHA VII

༄ བླ་མ་རིན་པོ་ཆེ་མཚུར་ཕུ་ངོས་བཟང་དགོན་པ་ན་བཞུགས་པའི་དུས་ན་བདེ་བ་ལྔའི་མགུར་···

One time when the precious guru was staying at the truly excellent gonpa, Tshurpu, he composed this "Doha of the Five Happinesses".

In the experiential space of emptiness, rigpa glides about and
There is not even the name "five poisonous causes" to be given[1]!
When the view has been settled on, mind is happy.

In the experiential space of non-duality, great bliss glides about and
There is not even the name "point of straying" to be given!
When the meditation has been settled on, mind is happy.

In the experiential space of non-birth, automatic occurrence[2] glides about and
There is not even the name "stopping, creating" to be given!
When the conduct has been settled on, mind is happy!

In the experiential space of wisdom, dharmakaya glides about and
There is not even the name "this life and later ones" to be given!
When the fruition has been settled on, mind is happy!

In the experiential space of the conqueror's realm, automatic occurrence glides about and
There is not even the name "getting more closely connected" to be given!
When one's own country has been settled on, mind is happy!

Notes:

1. Five poisonous causes are the five main afflictions of mind—desire, anger, ignorance, pride, and jealousy. Afflictions are the direct cause of further existence within samsara. Rigpa is the opposite of the afflictions.

2. "Automatic occurrence" means that things just happen as they do; it implies an absence of conceptual mind and its attempts to orchestrate the events of the universe.

DOHA VIII

The precious one, when staying at a sacred place at the time of doing the full moon Delta Scorpio[1] offering, said this.

"Yesterday at the time of Delta Scorpio's full moon,
In commemoration of the Lord's[2] passing
We did the offering to the three[3];
That evening, I supplicated the Lord.

In a dream during the early dawn
I thought that I the Jetsun[4] had come before me;
The lord said this to me.
"Understand view to be rigpa free from extremes,
Understand meditation to be the innate without change,
Understand conduct to be a peaceful mind without
attachment,
Understand fruition to the those three inseparable;
Just that is how factual dharmakaya functions[5].
Now, perform enlightened activity for other's sakes like
this:
Perform generosity as absence of clinging,

Protect discipline as absence of harm,
Cultivate patience as absence of anger,
Undertake perseverance as absence of idleness,
Cultivate absorption as absence of distraction,
Rouse wisdom as great bliss free from elaborations,
Dedicate those six for the sake of migrators."
That is what I heard him say.

❁ ❁ ❁

The precious guru said this while staying at a sacred place.[6]

"Namo Guru.

I'm a person for whom samsara and nirvana are a non-duality so
Shouldn't I be free from both hope and fear?
I'm a person for whom the yidam exists as mind's appearance
Shouldn't I be working on Development and Completion meditations[7]?
I'm a person for whom obstacles are accomplishment so
Shouldn't I be working on protection circle and recitation[8]?
I'm a person for whom wind and mind exist as a non-duality so
Shouldn't I be working on channel and wind meditation?
I'm a person for whom faults themselves are good qualities, so
Shouldn't I be cutting the points of deviation of experiences?

I'm a person who comes from appearance and mind
merged so
Shouldn't I be free of dualized grasped-grasping?
I'm a person for whom self and other are non-dual so
Shouldn't I be free of attachment and aversion?
I'm a person on the peak where there are no further births
so
Shouldn't I pass through the levels and paths in one life?
I'm a person of primordial spontaneous-existence so
Shouldn't I be free of cause and condition[9]?
I'm a person of the Middle Way between both existence
and non-existence so
Shouldn't I be beyond rational mind?
I'm a person who comes from equipoise and post-
attainment merged so
Shouldn't I have stability of the practice of mind[10]?
I'm a person for whom conduct is the sixfold group let
loose[11] so
Shouldn't conceptual tokens be dealt with as one's own
mind liberated[12]?
I'm a person free of the pair virtuous and evil deeds so
With the four modes of behaviour[13] captured in their own
place,
Shouldn't it be it that I am free of conceited activity?
I'm a person in the state of the five sense objects being
illusion so
Shouldn't adventitious clinging have been reversed[14]?
I'm a person of luminosity without interruption so
Shouldn't it be that there are none of the three bardos for
me[15]?
I'm a person for whom everything has been determined as
mind so

Shouldn't I have the expertise of one thing liberating all[16]?
It is not necessary to be concerning myself with a
composition of words;
I should be getting on with my cookery of dharma,
shouldn't I?"

❁ ❁ ❁

And, when the precious guru was staying at White Lake, he said this[17].

"E MA
Seated in the charnel ground of this corpse of a body,
Is mindness, the self-arising king;
Before it was propelled by discursive thought,
Now it has the great bliss fact[18].
Its jewel, the rigpa minister,
Before broken up in the space of thought process,
Now as rigpa, knows all of self and other.
The eight dharmas that are part of samsara
Before were emitted for each respective object,
Now they assemble in the land of non-separation[19].
The alaya grandmother with its thousands of daughters
Before was clothed with the faults of loose discipline,
Now it is mindness captured in its own place[20].
The steed of mind which without traces[21]
Which before raced along the wrong path
Now is held with the reigns of the authentic[22].
Mindness the precious gem

Which fefore was broken apart, present only in the cracks
between afflictions,
Now is captured in its own peace.
Reliance on the ground is such a joyful experience!
Reliance on its fact brings such mirth[23]!"

❁ ❁ ❁

The precious Jetsun was staying at Phom Cave. When a geshe from Central Tibet asked him some questions, this sprung forth[24]:

"Self-knowing realized free of extremes
Is understood to be the ultimate of view;
Does someone involved in tenets have a bit of it[25]?
Abiding un-interruptedly in the innate[26]
Is understood to be the ultimate of meditation;
Does someone involved in placement here and there have a
bit of it[27]?
Body and mind dedicated for the sake of migrators
Is understood to be the ultimate of conduct;
Does someone who has his own sake at heart have a bit of
it[28]?
When those three have been realized as an inseparable one
That is understood to be the ultimate of fruition;
Does someone with hopes and fears have a bit of it?[29]
That, Mr. Central Tibet, is the meaning of meditation isn't
it?![30]
If you realize that, it is the ultimate!

What he said was said via the four things of view, meditation, conduct, and fruition.

Notes:

1. Delta Scorpio is the seventeenth of the twenty-eight constellations used in ancient Indian astrology for calculating the lunar month. The Indian name is Anurādhā.

2. His guru, Gampopa.

3. Probably the Three Jewels.

4. His guru, Gampopa.

5. Factual dharmakaya is the dharmakaya known to mind as a fact, as opposed to the conceptual understanding that the words just spoken generate. This and the next line have the sense of, "Well, you have that sort of dharmakaya functioning in you because of your realization now use it to benefit sentient beings like this."

6. This doha runs by one line stating the view that he follows according to his guru's instructions and the second line stating how he should be if he is following that instruction. The last two lines say, "Enough of this verbal composition! I need to get on with cooking up actual dharma, not words about it!"

7. These are the two main phases of meditation of the Vajra Vehicle, which is what he practises.

8. Protection circle and recitation are aspects of yidam practice.

9. Spontaneous existence as opposed to existence produced by karmic causes and conditions is how phenomena come into existence in the enlightened realm. Spontaneous existence is free of those karmic causes and conditions.

10. Equipoise and post-attainment cover all possibilities of meditation.

11. The six-fold group is the human consciousness as a single group, which is comprised of six consciousnesses, those of mind and the five physical senses. Letting them loose is a particular practice of Mahamudra in which they are left untouched, allowed to dangle loosely, so to speak, just as they are.

12. Conceptual tokens are the stuff of conceptual mind that lets it operate. Normally, we relate to sense appearances by the names of concepts, which are these conceptual tokens. If one is to relate to appearances according to the Mahamudra instruction, all dualistic mind, including its tokens, has to be taken into mind that has been liberated from grasping at a self. When that is done, it is possible to have the names for the appearances without the fault of saṃsāric dualism.

13. Staying and going, sitting and walking.

14. Sentient beings cling on to the consciousnesses of the senses as they arise. This clinging just comes up and goes away. The yogin defeats the clinging and the consciousnesses are freed into being known as illusory.

15. Naropa's Six Dharmas include bardo instructions. Those bardo instructions explain three phases of the bardo after death that are places where one can be liberated from samsara. Those are the three bardos being referred to here.

16. The whole point of the oral instruction that all things are mind is to go to the end-point of the instruction which is to realize dharmakaya. When you realize dharmakaya in Mahamudra, it is called "knowing one liberates all". Here he has made a play on that; if everything is mind, then by going to the end of that, which is dharmakaya, then he should be expert in everything.

17. The thrust of this song is mindness and how it was wild before but now has been brought back to itself and is peace.

18. The actual fact of dharmakaya which has great bliss with it.

19. The key instruction that Dusum Khyenpa's guru Gampopa was famous for was the instruction that all thoughts are dharmakaya. In that approach, the thoughts of the eight worldly dharmas are not eliminated but are taken into mind that is included within mindness. In that way, thoughts lose their saṃsāric power and are part of the vast plain of mindness. It is not, according to Gampopa, that there is no thought process at all. This point is tricky and this here is a very brief explanation of it.

20. Mindness before was the ālaya consciousness, the repository of the countless seeds, virtuous and non-virtuous, that gave rise to all future events for that mind. It is no longer the recipient of those seeds because the alaya has been purified into mindness.

21. Without harness and reigns, and so on that could be used to control it. In other words, it was uncontrolled.

22. The authentic is a name for actuality, reality as it is.

23. Again, fact has the meaning of the actual fact of the thing known directly in mind, not the words or the concepts pointed to by words.

24. The geshe would have been a Kadampa Geshe from one of the several large groups who lived in Central Tibet, possibly from one of the Kadampa enclaves that Dusum Khyenpa's guru, Gampopa, spent so much time with. The geshes had a very conceptual, sutra-based approach to meditation, even though they did do Secret Mantra practice. The song criticizes the geshe as being that type of a person and points out that his approach to dharma is disconnected from dharma that is reality.

25. Tenets here meaning conceptual approaches to reality using philosophical tenets. He is berating the geshe in each of four

steps corresponding to the four aspects of ground, path, conduct, and fruition. The geshe from central Tibet, as with so many geshes, apparently was just stuck in concept. In those times, geshe was synonymous with Kadampa expert. Milarepa often criticised the Kadampas in this way. His main disciple Gampopa, who started out as a Kadampa expert but who gained real attainment after practising with Milarepa did, too. Dusum Khyenpa's style reflects that of his teachers.

26. The innate is the essence of mind. It is a name for buddha mind when the practitioner is still on the path.

27. The Kadampa geshe's approach to meditation would emphasis placement of mind on this or that, which is still a worldly type of samadhi.

28. He is saying that the Kadampa geshe might have all the words of bodhichitta, which the Kadampa's were very strong on, but that he had not taken them to heart. Dusum Khyenpa on the other hand had ultimate bodhichitta beyond all conceptual trainings in bodhichitta.

29. Hope and fear is a sign of samsaric mind. For as long as you have that, you do not have the ultimate fruition in which samsaric mind has utterly collapsed for once and for all.

30. Central Tibet was the home of the Kadamapa geshes and apparently this man was from Central Tibet.

GLOSSARY

Actuality, Tib. gnas lugs: how things are, the way things are, how things sit in any given situation as opposed to how they might appear.

Adventitious, Tib. glo bur: Often translated as "sudden", the word "adventitious" in English more accurately reflects the full meaning of the original Tibetan. Something adventitious is something which suddenly comes up as a surface event and disappears again in regard to something else since it does not belong to the core of the thing that it appeared on the surface of.

Affliction, Skt. kleśha, Tib. nyon mongs: this term is usually translated as emotion or disturbing emotion, etcetera. However, the Buddha was much more specific about the meaning of this word. When the Buddha described the emotions, he called them "kleśha" in Sanskrit, meaning that they were afflictions. Buddha did not talk about "emotion" meaning a movement of mind but specifically used the term "affliction". He explained that they afflict you, giving you problems. This is one of many terms that has lost most of its meaning by its common mistranslation.

Alaya, Tib. kun gzhi: this term, if translated, is usually translated as all-base or thereabouts. It means a range that underlies something else; an underlying basis for something else. It is used in several different ways in the Buddhist teaching and changes to a different meaning in case. All in all, it means a space of mind that underlies many other minds that come from it.

Clinging, Tib. zhen pa: dualistic mind that takes things that are not true, not pure, as being true, pure, etcetera and then, because of seeing them as highly desirable attaches itself or clings to those things. It acts a kind of glue that keeps you with the things of cyclic existence, such as thoughts.

Confusion, Tib. 'khrul pa: the Tibetan term means fundamental delusion's confusion of taking things the wrong way. This is not the other meaning in English of having lots of thoughts and being confused about it. It is much more fundamental than that. The definition in Tibetan is "confusion is the appearance to rational mind of something being present when it is not" and refers for example to seeing any object, such as a table, as being truly present when in fact it is present only as mere appearance which has occurred in a process of dependent, related arising.

Contrivance, contrived, Tib. bcos pa: something which has been altered from its native state or the process of making that alteration.

Cyclic existence, Tib. 'khor ba: saṃsāra: the type of existence that sentient beings have which is that continue on from one existence to another, always within the enclosure of births that are produced by ignorance and experienced as unsatisfactory.

Dharmakaya, Tib. chos sku: the mind aspect of a buddha which, in the Thorough Cut system, is the fruition level of rigpa.

Dharmata, Tib. chos nyid: literally dharma-ness. A dharma is a phenomenon so what it is at core, its actual reality is its dharma-ness, or its isness.

Discursive thought, Tib. rnam rtog: this means more than just the superficial thought that is heard as a voice in the head. It includes the entirety of conceptual process that arises due to mind contacting any object of any of the senses. Discursive thought here translates from the Sanskrit original where the meaning is "conceptual thought that arises from the mind wandering among the various superficies perceived in the doors of the senses".

Equipoise and post-attainment, Tib. mnyam bzhag and rjes thob: often mis-translated as meditation and post-meditation, "equipoise and post-attainment" is a correct rendering. There is great meaning in the words and that meaning is lost by the looser translation. Note that equipoise and post-attainment are used throughout the three vehicles and that they have a very different meaning in Great Completion than in lower vehicles.

Essence, Tib. ngo bo: a key term used throughout Buddhist theory. The original in Sanskrit and the term in Tibetan, too, has both meanings of "essence" and "entity". In some situations the term has more the first meaning and in others, the second. For example, when speaking of mind and mind's essence, it is referring to the core or essential part within mind. On the other hand, when speaking of fire or some other thing, there is the entity, fire, and so on, and its characteristics, such as heat, and so on; in this case, it is not an essence but an entity.

Fictional Truth, Tib. kun rdzob bden pa: one of a pair of terms; the other is Superfactual Truth, q.v. The usual translation as "relative truth" is not the meaning at all of this key term. The term means the level of reality (*truth*) made up by the obscuration of an ordinary person's mind. Because this is an obscured version of actual truth it is *fictional*. However, it is true for the beings who make it up, so it is still called *truth*.

Foremost Instructions, Skt. upadeśha, Tib. man ngag: there are several types of instruction mentioned in Buddhist literature: there is the general level of instruction which is the meaning contained in the words of the texts of the tradition; on a more personal and direct level there is oral instruction which has been passed down from teacher to student from the time of the buddha; and on the most profound level there is upadesha which are oral instructions provided by one's guru which are the core instructions that come out of personal experience and which convey the teaching concisely and with the full weight of personal experience. Upadesha are crucial to the vajrayāna path because these are the special way of passing on the profound instructions needed for the student's realization.

Grasped-grasping, Tib. gzung 'dzin: When mind is turned outwardly as it is in the normal operation of dualistic mind, it has developed two faces that appear simultaneously. Special names are given to these two faces: mind appearing in the form of the external object being referenced is called "that which is grasped". Mind appearing in the form of the consciousness that is referencing it is called "the grasper" or "grasping" of it. Thus, there is the pair of terms "grasped-grasper" or "grasped-grasping". When these two terms are used, it alerts you immediately to the fact that a Mind Only style of presentation is being discussed and it should bring the whole flavour of Mind Only along with it. This pair of terms pervades Mind Only, Madhyamaka, and tantric writings and is exceptionally important in all of them.

The solidified duality of grasped and grasper is nothing but an invention of dualistic thought. It has that kind of character or characteristic.

Note that you could substitute the word "apprehended" for "grasped" and "apprehender" for "grasper" or "grasping" and that would reflect one connotation of the original Indian terminology.

Great Vehicle, Skt. mahāyāna, Tib. theg pa chen po: The Buddha's teachings as a whole can be summed up into three vehicles where a vehicle is defined as that which can carry you to a certain destination. The first vehicle, called the Lesser Vehicle, contains the teachings designed to get an individual moving on the spiritual path through showing the unsatisfactory state of cyclic existence and an emancipation from that. The path shown though is only concerned with a personal emancipation and fails to take account of all of the beings that there are in existence. There used to be eighteen schools of Lesser Vehicle in India but the only one surviving these days is the Theravada of south-east Asia. The Greater Vehicle is a step up from that. The Buddha explained that it was great in comparison to the Lesser Vehicle for seven reasons. The first of those is that it is concerned with truly complete enlightenment of a truly complete buddha for the sake of every sentient being where the Lesser Vehicle is only concerned with a personal liberation that is not truly complete enlightenment and which is only achieved for the sake of that practitioner. The Great Vehicle has two divisions. There is a conventional Great Vehicle in which the path is taught in a logical, conventional way. There is also an unconventional Great Vehicle in which the path is taught in an unconventional and very direct way. This latter vehicle is called the Vajra Vehicle because it relies on showing the innermost, indestructible (vajra) fact of reality of one's own mind. The teachings in this book, while they do go through the Lesser and conventional Great Vehicles are principally concerned with the Vajra Vehicle.

Isness: Tib. a translation of dharmatā, q.v.

Luminosity, Skt. prabhāsvara, Tib. 'od gsal ba: the core of mind, called mind's essence, has two aspects, parts, or factors as they are called. One is emptiness and the other is knowing. Luminosity is a metaphor for the fundamental knowing quality of the essence of mind. It is sometimes translated as "clear light" but that is a mistake that comes from not understanding how the words of the Tibetan go together. It does not refer to a light that is clear but refers to the illuminative property which is the hallmark of mind. Mind knows, that is what it does. Thus, it has the property of luminosity which knows its own content. Both in Sanskrit and Tibetan Buddhist literature, the term is frequently abbreviated just to gsal ba, "clarity", with the same meaning.

Mind, Tib. sems: conventional minding which occurs because there is ignorance.

Prajña, Tib. shes rab: a name for a state of mind that makes precise distinctions between this and that. Although it is sometimes translated as "wisdom", that is not correct because it is, generally speaking, a mental event belonging to dualistic mind.

Rational mind, Tib. blo: the Kagyu and Nyingma traditions use this term pejoratively for the most part. In the Great Completion tradition, blo is the dualistic mind and hence is the villain so to speak which needs to be removed from the equation in order to obtain enlightenment. This term is consistently translated as rational mind throughout this text since merely translating it as mind, which is the common approach these days, utterly loses the importance of the word. This is not just mind but this is the mind that creates the situation of this and that (ratio in latin) and which is always at the root of all sentient beings problems and which is the very opposite of the mind of rigpa. This is a key term and it should be noted and not just glossed over as "mind".

Rigpa, Tib. rig pa: the key words of key words in the system of Mahamudra. Rigpa literally means to know in the sense of "I see!" It is used at all levels of meaning from the coarsest everyday sense of knowing something to the deepest sense of knowing something as presented in the system of Mahamudra. The system of Mahamudra uses this term in a very special sense, though it still retains its basic meaning of "to know". To translate it as "awareness" which is common practice these days is a poor practice; there are many kinds of awareness but there is only one rigpa and besides, rigpa is substantially more than just awareness. Since this is such an important term and since it lacks an equivalent in English, I choose not to translate it. However, it will be helpful in reading the text to understanding the meaning as just given.

Secret Mantra, Tib. gsang sngags: the name for the second of the two parts of the Mahāyāna school, that is, the vajrayāna.

State, Tib. ngang: this is a key term in Mahāmudrā and Great Completion. Unfortunately it is often not translated or is simply translated as "within". It has the full sense of "a particular state that the practitioner is experiencing". There are many states on the path. The word is often used in the Thorough Cut without adjective to refer to the all-important experience of rigpa itself, whatever that might be at the time. Hence "the state", "preserving the state", etcetera. See also "Preserve".

Superfactual Truth, Tib. don dam bden pa: one of a pair of terms; the other is Fictional Truth, q.v. The usual translation as "absolute truth" is not the meaning at all of this key term. The term means the level of reality(*truth*) which is *superior* to the ordinary person's mistaken kind of reality and which is *factual* compared to the fictional reality of the ordinary person.

Superfice, superficies, Tib. rnam pa: in discussions of mind, a distinction is made between the entity of mind which is a mere knower and the superficial things that appear on its surface and which are known by it. In other words, the superficies are the various things which pass over the surface of mind but which are not mind. Superficies are all the specifics that constitute appearance, for example, the colour white within a moment of visual consciousness, the vroom of a motorbike within an ear consciousness, and so on.

Unaltered or uncontrived, Tib. ma bcos pa: the opposite of "altered" and "contrived". Something which has not been altered from its native state. Something which has been left just as it is.

Upadesha, Tib. man ngag: see "foremost instructions".

Wisdom, Tib. ye shes: this terms translates the original Sanskrit, jñāna. Jñāna has many meanings but overall has the sense of just knowing. In the Buddhist usage it is very literal, meaning the most basic sense we have of knowing which is the knowing that is there from the beginning in the core of mind. Because of this meaning, the Tibetans translated it as "the particular awareness which has been there from the beginning". This has been translated into English in various ways but, as long as the meaning just mentioned is understood, that will be enough.

In the tantras, there are many methods for bringing the students to this primordial awareness. Some of them bring the student first to something which is similar to the wisdom so there is the term, simile wisdom[1]; this is often translated as example wisdom but that is being literal to the extent of losing the meaning. The simile wisdom is a similitude of the real wisdom, the actual wisdom which is shown in various

---

[1] Tib. dpe'i ye shes

ways, including by the fourth empowerment. Real wisdom[2] is the opposite of simile wisdom; it is wisdom in fact, not the one which is just a similitude of the real wisdom.

---

[2] Tib. don gyi ye shes